GAO

Report to the Chairman, Subcommittee on Government Management, Information and Technology, Committee on Government Reform, House of Representatives

September 2000

INFORMATION SECURITY

I0410971

Serious and Widespread Weaknesses Persist at Federal Agencies

GAO

Accountability ★ Integrity ★ Reliability

GAO/AIMD-00-295

September   ,

The Honorable Stephen Horn
Chairman, Subcommittee on Government Management,
   Information and Technology
Committee on Government Reform
House of Representatives

   ear Mr Chairman

This report responds to your   uly   ,   , re uest that   e summari e the
results of recent information security audits at federal agencies   ike other
large organi ations, federal agencies rely e tensively on computeri ed
systems and electronic data to support their missions Accordingly, the
security of these systems and data is essential to help avoid disruptions in
critical operations, data tampering, fraud, and inappropriate disclosures of
confidential information

This report summari es audit findings for the   federal agencies that   ere
included in a similar revie   that   e reported on in September
agencies that, during fiscal year   , accounted for almost   percent of
federal outlays In our   report,   e concluded that significant computer
security   eaknesses had been reported for each of those agencies and that,
as a result, critical federal operations and assets   ere at risk

In accordance   ith your re uest, our ob ectives   ere to   analy e and
summari e information security   eaknesses identified in audit reports
issued from   uly   through August   and compare our findings   ith
similar information that   e reported in September   ,   identify
e amples of   eaknesses and the related risks at selected individual
agencies, and   identify the most significant types of   eaknesses in each
of si   categories of general controls that   e used in our analysis The
agency audit reports   e analy ed, most of   hich are referenced
throughout this report,   ere produced primarily by us and agency
inspectors general IG

Information Security Serious Weaknesses Place Critical Federal Operations and Assets at
Risk GAO AIM   , September   ,

Results in Brief

Evaluations of computer security published since July continue to show that federal computer security is fraught with weaknesses and that, as a result, critical operations and assets continue to be at risk As in , our current analysis identified significant weaknesses in each of the agencies covered by our review Since July , the range of weaknesses in individual agencies has broadened, at least in part because the scope of audits being performed is more comprehensive than in prior years While these audits are providing a more complete picture of the security problems agencies face, they also show that agencies have much work to do to ensure that their security programs are complete and effective

The weaknesses identified place a broad array of federal operations and assets at risk of fraud, misuse, and disruption For example, weaknesses at the Department of the Treasury increase the risk of fraud associated with billions of dollars of federal payments and collections, and weaknesses at the Department of Defense increase the vulnerability of various military operations that support the department s war fighting capability Further, information security weaknesses place enormous amounts of confidential data, ranging from personal and tax data to proprietary business information, at risk of inappropriate disclosure For example, in , a Social Security Administration employee pled guilty to unauthorized access of the administration s systems The related investigation determined that the employee had made many unauthorized queries, including obtaining earnings information for members of the local business community

For most agencies, the weaknesses reported covered the full range of computer security controls For example, security program planning and management were inadequate Physical and logical access controls also were not effective in preventing or detecting system intrusions and misuse In addition, software change controls were ineffective in ensuring that only properly authorized and tested software programs were implemented Further, duties were not adequately segregated to reduce the risk that one individual could execute unauthorized transactions or software changes without detection Finally, sensitive operating system software was not adequately controlled, and adequate steps had not been taken to ensure continuity of computerized operations

We and agency inspectors general have made scores of recommendations to agencies regarding specific steps they should take to make their security programs more effective Most agencies have heeded these recommendations and taken at least some corrective actions However, more needs to be done, especially in the area of security program planning and management, hich involves instituting routine risk management activities aimed at ensuring that risks are understood, that appropriate controls are implemented commensurate ith risk, and that these controls operate as intended

ackground

ramatic increases in computer interconnectivity, especially in use of the Internet, are revolutioni ing the ay our government, our nation, and much of the orld communicate and conduct business The benefits have been enormous ast amounts of information are no literally at our fingertips, facilitating research on virtually every topic imaginable financial and other business transactions can be e ecuted almost instantaneously, often on a hour a day basis and electronic mail, Internet Web sites, and computer bulletin boards allo us to communicate uickly and easily ith a virtually unlimited number of other individuals and groups

Ho ever, in addition to its benefits, this idespread interconnectivity poses significant risks to our computer systems and, more importantly, to the critical operations and infrastructures they support, such as telecommunications po er distribution national defense, including the military s arfighting capability la enforcement government services and emergency services The same factors that benefit operations speed and accessibility if not properly controlled, also make it possible for individuals and organi ations to ine pensively interfere ith or eavesdrop on these operations from remote locations for purposes of fraud or sabotage, or for other malicious or mischievous purposes isruptions caused by recent virus attacks, such as the I O EYOU virus in May and s Melissa virus, have illustrated the potential for damage that such attacks hold In addition, natural disasters and inadvertent errors by authori ed computer users can have devastating conse uences if information resources are poorly protected

Critical Infrastructure Protection I O EYOU Computer irus Highlights Need for Improved Alert and Coordination Capabilities GAO T AIM , May ,
Information Security I O EYOU Computer irus Emphasi es Critical Need for Agency and Government ide Improvements GAO T AIM , May , *Information Security The Melissa Computer irus emonstrates Urgent Need for Stronger Protection over Systems and Sensitive ata* GAO T AIM , April ,

Government officials are increasingly concerned about attacks from individuals and groups ith malicious intentions, such as crime, terrorism, foreign intelligence gathering, and acts of ar According to the Federal ureau of Investigation F I , terrorists, transnational criminals, and intelligence services are uickly becoming a are of and using information e ploitation tools such as computer viruses, Tro an Horses, orms, logic bombs, and eavesdropping sniffers that can destroy, intercept, or degrade the integrity of and deny access to data As greater amounts of money are transferred through computer systems, as more sensitive economic and commercial information is e changed electronically, and as the nation s defense and intelligence communities increasingly rely on commercially available information technology, there is a greater likelihood that information attacks ill threaten vital national interests

While complete summary data are not available because many computer security incidents are not reported, the number of incidents that are reported is gro ing For e ample, the number of reported incidents handled by Carnegie Mellon University s CERT Coordination Center has increased from , in to , during the first t o uarters of Similarly, the Federal ureau of Investigation reports that its case load of computer intrusion related cases is more than doubling every year The fifth annual survey conducted by the Computer Security Institute in cooperation ith the F I found that percent of respondents primarily large corporations and government agencies had detected serious computer security breaches ithin the last months and that uantifiable financial losses had increased over past years

Our previous analyses have sho n that federal agency systems ere not being ade uately protected from these threats, even though these systems process, store, and transmit enormous amounts of sensitive data and are indispensable to many federal agency operations In September , e

---

Originally called the Computer Emergency Response Team, the center as established in by the efense Advanced Research Pro ects Agency It is charged ith establishing a capability to uickly and effectively coordinate communication among e perts in order to limit the damage associated ith, and respond to, incidents and building a areness of security issues across the Internet community

Issues and Trends CSI F I Computer Crime and Security Survey, The Computer Security Institute, March

reported that serious eaknesses had been reported for of the largest federal agencies In that report e concluded that poor information security as a idespread federal problem ith potentially devastating conse uences, and, in and reports to the Congress, e identified information security as a high risk issue In , e analy ed audit results for of the largest federal agencies and reported that all of them had significant information security eaknesses

The primary responsibility for implementing ade uate security lies ith individual agencies Officials in these agencies are most familiar ith the agency programs and assets that are at risk, and, therefore, they are in the best position to determine hat operations and assets merit the strongest protection and control and ensure that security programs are effective on an ongoing basis Accordingly, improvements must be implemented at the individual agency level

Centrally directed government ide efforts to improve federal information security are also important to provide central policy direction and address issues that affect multiple agencies Several such efforts are under ay, many as part of broader efforts to protect our nation s critical computer support infrastructures Most recently, in anuary , the President issued the National Plan for Information Systems Protection, hich called for ne initiatives to strengthen the nation s defenses against threats to public and private sector critical information systems In addition, the federal Chief Information Officers Council and others have several pro ects under ay that are intended to promote and support information security improvements

Information Security Opportunities for Improved OM Oversight of Agency Practices GAO AIM , September ,

High Risk Series Information Management and Technology GAO HR , February , , High Risk Series An Update GAO HR , anuary

Information Security Serious Weaknesses Place Critical Federal Operations and Assets at Risk GAO AIM , September ,

efending America s Cyberspace *National Plan for Information Systems Protection ersion An Invitation to a ialogue,* released anuary , , The White House

Weaknesses Remain Pervasive

As in our   analysis, audit reports issued since uly   identified significant information security eaknesses in each of the   agencies covered by our analysis Also, as in   , eaknesses ere reported in all si ma or areas of general controls that e used to categori e them General controls are the policies, procedures, and technical controls that apply to all or a large segment of an entity s information systems and help ensure their proper operation These eaknesses placed a broad range of critical operations and assets at risk for fraud, misuse, and disruption In addition, they placed an enormous amount of highly sensitive data, much of it on individual ta payers and beneficiaries, at risk of inappropriate disclosure

Table   provides an overvie   of the types of eaknesses reported throughout the government, as ell as the gaps in audit coverage

Table 1: Areas of Information Security Weakness Reported for 24 Federal Agencies

General control area	Number of agencies					
	Significant weakness identified		No significant weakness identified		Area not reviewed	
	1998	2000	1998	2000	1998	2000
Entitywide security program planning and management	17	21	0	0	7	3
Access controls	23	24	0	0	1	0
Application software development and change controls	14	19	4	2	6	3
Segregation of duties	16	17	1	3	7	4
System software controls	9	18	0	0	15	6
Service continuity controls	20	20	0	1	4	3

As in   , the most idely audited area and the area here eaknesses ere most often identified   as access controls Weak controls over access to sensitive data and systems make it possible for an individual or group to inappropriately modify, destroy, or disclose sensitive data or computer programs for purposes such as personal gain or sabotage In today s increasingly interconnected computing environment, poor access controls can e pose an agency s information and operations to attacks from remote locations all over the world by individuals with minimal computer and telecommunications resources and expertise

Many problems were also identified in the area of entity wide security program planning and management an area that is fundamental to the appropriate selection and effectiveness of the other categories of controls Security program planning and management cover a range of activities related to understanding information security risks selecting and implementing controls commensurate with risk and ensuring that controls, once implemented, continue to operate effectively

One notable change since September is that the scope of audit work performed has expanded to more fully cover all six ma or areas of general controls at each agency Not surprisingly, this has led to identification of additional areas of weakness at some agencies and an overall increase in the number of agencies with significant weaknesses identified in five of the six general control categories While these increases in reported weaknesses are disturbing, they do not necessarily mean that information security at federal agencies is getting worse It is more likely that they sho that information security weaknesses are becoming more fully understood an important step to ard addressing the overall problem Nevertheless, the numbers in table leave no doubt that serious weaknesses are pervasive

As auditors increase their proficiency and the body of audit evidence expands, it is probable that additional significant deficiencies will be identified Most of the audits used to develop table were performed as part of financial statement audits At some agencies with primarily financial missions, such as the epartment of the Treasury and the Social Security Administration, these audits covered the bulk of mission related operations Ho ever, at other agencies hose missions are primarily nonfinancial, such as the epartments of efense and ustice, the audits used to develop this table may provide a less complete picture of the agency s overall security posture because the audit ob ectives focused on the financial statements and did not include evaluating systems supporting nonfinancial operations In response to congressional interest, during fiscal year and , e e panded our audit focus to cover a ider range of nonfinancial operations, a trend that is likely to continue

E amples of Weaknesses at Individual Agencies Highlight Risks to Operations, Assets, Confidentiality

To understand the significance of the eaknesses summari ed in table , it is necessary to link them to the risks they present to federal operations and assets irtually all federal operations are supported by automated systems and electronic data, and agencies ould find it difficult, if not impossible, to carry out their missions and account for their resources ithout these information assets Reported eaknesses and the significant risks they pose to critical federal operations are described belo

epartment of the Treasury

The epartment of the Treasury hich includes the Internal Revenue Service U S Customs Service ureau of the Public ebt Financial Management Service and ureau of Alcohol, Tobacco, and Firearms relies on computer systems to process, collect or disburse, and account for over trillion in federal receipts and payments annually In addition, the department s computers handle enormous amounts of highly sensitive data associated ith ta payer records, la enforcement operations, and support operations critical to financing the federal government, maintaining the flo of benefits to individuals and organi ations, and controlling imports and e ports

Although protecting these operations and assets is essential to the elfare of our nation, in February , the Treasury IG reported that absence of effective general controls over computer based financial systems at certain Treasury components continued to be a material eakness in the department s internal controls The IG report e plained that this absence of controls makes the department vulnerable to losses, fraud, delays, and interruptions in service In addition, it compromises the integrity and reliability of the department s information systems and data

Weaknesses for specific Treasury bureaus include the follo ing

In October , e reported that pervasive computer security eaknesses at Treasury s Financial Management Service placed billions of dollars of payments and collections at significant risk of loss or fraud, vast amounts of sensitive data at risk of inappropriate disclosure, and

Report on the epartment of the Treasury s Fiscal Year Financial Statements OIG , February ,

critical computer based operations at risk of serious disruption These
 eaknesses affected a ide array of information systems that the
Financial Management Service uses in its role as the government s
central financial manager, disburser, and collection agency

In February   , e reported that significant eaknesses in the
Internal Revenue Service s IRS computer security controls continued
to place ta payer and other data in IRS automated systems at serious
risk of unauthori ed disclosure, modification, or destruction
Specifically, IRS continued to have serious eaknesses ith general
controls designed to protect computing resources such as net orks,
computer e uipment, soft are programs, data, and facilities from
unauthori ed use, modification, loss, and disclosure IRS did not al ays
    effectively implement controls to prevent, limit, or detect access to
computing resources,   ade uately segregate system administration
and security administration responsibilities,   optimally configure
system soft are to ensure the integrity of system programs, files, and
data,   sufficiently plan or test the activities re uired to restore critical
business systems   hen une pected events occur, and   routinely
monitor key net orks and systems to identify unauthori ed activities
and inappropriate system configurations

In February   , the Treasury IG reported significant deficiencies in the
Customs Service s ability to provide for the timely restoration of
mission critical systems that could impair Customs ability to respond
effectively to a disruption in operations   The Treasury IG determined
that Customs had not established a frame ork to assess risk, developed
and implemented effective security procedures, or monitored the
effectiveness of these procedures on a continuous basis In addition, the
IG identified eaknesses in Customs logical access controls over its
data files, application programs, and computer related facilities,
e uipment, and infrastructure Weaknesses in controls over computer
based financial systems makes Customs vulnerable to losses, delays, or

Financial Management Service Significant Weaknesses in Computer Controls
GAO AIM   , October ,

Financial Audit IRS Fiscal Year   Financial Statements GAO AIM   ,
February ,   Also see *IRS Systems Security Although Improvements Made, Ta*
Processing Operations and   ata Still at Serious Risk GAO AIM   , ecember ,

Report on the   epartment of the Treasury s Fiscal Year   Financial Statements
OIG   , February ,

interruptions in service, and compromise the integrity and reliability of the information systems and data

Numerous recommendations have been made to Treasury bureaus over the years to correct these eaknesses, and many corrective actions are under ay In particular, IRS has made notable progress in improving computer security at its facilities and has corrected a significant number of the computer security eaknesses identified in our previous reports Also, IRS has established a service ide computer security management program that should, hen fully implemented, help the agency effectively manage its security risks

epartment of efense

The epartment of efense O   relies on a vast and comple computeri ed information infrastructure to support virtually all aspects of its operations, including strategic and tactical operations, eaponry, intelligence, and security This reliance e tends to its business operations that support the department, including financial management

Evaluations of the security of O   systems since uly   have continued to identify eaknesses that could seriously eopardi e operations and compromise the confidentiality, integrity, or availability of sensitive information In August   , e reported that serious eaknesses in O information security continued to provide both hackers and hundreds of thousands of authori ed users the opportunity to modify, steal, inappropriately disclose, and destroy sensitive O   data These eaknesses impaired O s ability to   control physical and electronic access to its systems and data,   ensure that soft are running on its systems is properly authori ed, tested, and functioning as intended,   limit employees ability to perform incompatible functions, and   resume operations in the event of a disaster As a result, numerous O functions including eapons and supercomputer research, logistics, finance, procurement, personnel management, military health, and payroll   had already been adversely affected by system attacks or fraud In May   , e had reported that attackers had stolen, modified, and destroyed both data and soft are at O   and installed back doors that circumvented normal system protection and allo ed attackers

---

O   Information Security Serious Weaknesses Continue to Place   efense Operations at Risk GAO AIM   , August   ,

unauthori ed future access   They had also shut do n and crashed entire systems and net orks

In our August   report, e stated that some corrective actions had been initiated in response to recommendations e made in   to address pervasive information security   eaknesses in O Ho ever, progress in correcting specific control   eaknesses identified in   and in previous revie s had been inconsistent across the various O components Although many factors contribute to these   eaknesses, audits by us and the O IG have found that an underlying cause of eak information security is poor management of security programs In August   , e reiterated this finding, as   ell as our recommendation that O   take steps to strengthen department ide security program management

In May   , e testified that the preliminary results of a recent revie   of the department s financial management systems sho ed that serious   eaknesses in access controls and systems soft are continued to e ist   uring that revie , e gained access to sensitive information through a file that   as publicly available over the Internet and,   ithout valid user authentication, gained access to employees social security numbers, addresses, and pay information, as   ell as budget, e penditure, and procurement information on pro ects At the close of this revie , the responsible O component   as taking corrective actions

O   has been taking steps to improve the department s information security Notably, the department has established the   efense ide Information Assurance Program under the urisdiction of the O Chief Information Officer and   oint Task Force for Computer Net ork   efense to monitor O computer net orks and defend against hacker attacks and other unauthori ed access We are currently revie ing these efforts

epartment of Energy

Information technology is essential to the   epartment of Energy s OE scientific research mission,   hich is supported by a large and diverse set of computing systems, including very po erful supercomputers, located at

---

Information Security Computer Attacks at   epartment of efense Pose Increasing Risks GAO AIM   , May   ,

epartment of   efense Progress in Financial Management Reform GAO T AIM   NSIA   , May   ,

OE laboratories across the nation Much of the research conducted at the laboratories is unclassified, and   OE officials have had to struggle to convince their user community that security threats are real and that effective security measures can be implemented that   ill not significantly constrain the openness they re uire to do scientific research

In une   , e reported that computer systems at   OE laboratories supporting civilian research had become a popular target of the hacking community   ith the result that the threat of attacks had gro n dramatically in recent years   We further noted that because of security breaches, several laboratories had been forced to temporarily disconnect their net orks from the Internet, disrupting the laboratories ability to do scientific research for up to a full   eek on at least t o occasions

In our report,   e stated that a ma or contributing factor to the e istence of   OE s security vulnerabilities   as that the department did not have an effective program for managing information technology security consistently throughout the department Specifically, during our revie , e found that   OE had not   prepared federally re uired security plans,   effectively identified and assessed information security risks,   provided ade uate policy guidance on   hat information   as appropriate for public Internet access,   effectively overseen implementation of computer security at the laboratories, and   fully and consistently reported security incidents

We recommended that the Secretary of Energy take specific actions to strengthen the management of the department s unclassified computer security program The department generally agreed   ith our recommendations and provided information on the actions it is taking

epartment of Health and Human Services

In February   , the   epartment of Health and Human Services HHS IG again reported serious control   eaknesses affecting the integrity, confidentiality, and availability of data maintained by the department Most significant   ere   eaknesses associated   ith the department s Health Care Financing Administration HCFA ,   hich, according to its reports,

---

Information Security   ulnerabilities in   OE s Systems for Unclassified Civilian Research GAO AIM   , une ,

Report on the Financial Statement Audit of the   epartment of Health and Human Services for Fiscal Year   , A   , February

as responsible, during fiscal year   , for processing health care claims for over   million beneficiaries and outlays of   billion   percent of total federal outlays

HCFA relies on e tensive data processing operations at its central office to maintain administrative data, such as Medicare enrollment, eligibility, and paid claims data, and to process all payments for managed care In fiscal year   , managed care payments totaled about   billion HCFA also relies on Medicare contractors,   ho use multiple shared systems to collect and process personal health, financial, and medical data associated   ith about   million Medicare claims annually

The IG s recent report identified many general control   eaknesses associated   ith computer controls at HCFAs central office, Medicare contractors, and the contractors shared systems At the central office,   eaknesses   ere identified in access controls, application soft are development and change controls, entity ide security program planning and management, and operating system soft are controls At Medicare contractors,   eaknesses   ere identified in these same areas plus   eaknesses in segregation of duties and service continuity Such   eaknesses increase the risk of   unauthori ed access to and disclosure of sensitive information,   malicious changes that could interrupt data processing or destroy data files,   improper Medicare payments, or   disruption of critical operations The report included many recommendations for addressing the identified   eaknesses

 oth HCFA and the Medicare contractors have taken steps to address previously reported   eaknesses In particular, the HCFA central office is planning for additional security soft are to restrict access to sensitive Medicare databases In addition, HHS has recogni ed the need to protect the security of information technology systems and the data contained in them, and the department continues to revise security policies and guidance and to re uire each ma or operating division to develop and implement corrective action plans to address unresolved   eaknesses Ho ever, serious   eaknesses persist

Social Security Administration

The Social Security Administration SSA relies on e tensive information processing resources to carry out its operations,   hich, for   , included payments that totaled   billion to more than   million beneficiaries, many of   hom rely on the uninterrupted flo of monthly payments to meet their basic needs This represents about   percent of the   trillion in federal e penditures The administration also issues social security numbers and maintains earnings records and other personal information on virtually all U S citi ens The public depends on SSA to protect trust fund revenues and assets from fraud and to protect sensitive information on individuals from inappropriate disclosure According to SSA, no other public program or public service entity directly touches the lives of so many people

In November , the SSA IG reported that SSAs systems environment remained threatened by eaknesses in several components of its information protection control structure The general areas here eaknesses ere noted ere entity ide security program planning and management and associated eaknesses in developing, implementing, and monitoring local area net orks and distributed systems security, SSAs mainframe computer security and operating system configuration, physical access controls at nonhead uarters locations, and certification and accreditation of certain general support and ma or application systems In addition, the IG reported that SSA needed to complete and fully test its plan for maintaining continuity of operations

According to the IG, until corrected, the eaknesses ill continue to increase the risks of unauthori ed access to, modification, or disclosure of sensitive SSA information These, in turn, increase the risks that data or SSA Trust Fund resources could be lost and that the privacy of information associated ith SSAs enumeration, earnings, retirement, and disability processes and programs could be compromised

Such eaknesses might allo an individual or group to fraudulently obtain payments by creating fictitious beneficiaries or increasing payment amounts Similarly, an individual or group might secretly obtain sensitive information and sell or other ise use it for personal gains In , a SSA employee pled guilty to unauthori ed access of SSAs systems from through November and, as part of a plea agreement, as re uired to pay , to SSA in restitution and resign from the agency This case as initiated based on an anonymous tip alleging that the SSA employee had accessed SSA records The IG confirmed the unauthori ed access and learned during the investigation that the SSA employee had made many other unauthori ed ueries, including obtaining earnings information for

Social Security Accountability Report for Fiscal Year , November ,

members of the local business community, such as a bank president, a pharmacist, a physician, an attorney, and a psychologist

In separate letters issued to SSA management, the IG and its contractor made recommendations to address the weaknesses reported in November SSA agreed with the majority of the recommendations in the SSA IG s report and agreed to develop related corrective action plans

Environmental Protection Agency

The Environmental Protection Agency EPA relies on its computer systems to collect and maintain a wealth of environmental data under various statutory and regulatory requirements EPA makes much of its information available to the public through Internet access in order to encourage public awareness and participation in managing human health and environmental risks and to meet statutory requirements EPA also maintains confidential data from private businesses, data of varying sensitivity on human health and environmental risks, financial and contract data, and personal information on its employees Consequently, EPAs information security program must accommodate the often competing goals of making much of its environmental information widely accessible while maintaining data integrity, availability, and appropriate confidentiality

In July , we reported serious and pervasive problems that essentially rendered EPAs agency wide information security program ineffective Our tests of computer based controls concluded that the computer operating systems and the agency wide computer network that support most of EPAs mission related and financial operations were riddled with security weaknesses Our report included over recommendations for correcting specific control weaknesses and strengthening EPAs agency wide security program

Of particular concern was that many of the most serious weaknesses we identified those related to inadequate protection from intrusions through the Internet and poor security planning had been previously reported to EPA management in by EPAs IG The negative effects of such

Information Security Fundamental Weaknesses Place EPA Data and Operations at Risk GAO AIM , uly ,

EPAs Internet Connectivity Controls, Office of Inspector General Report of Audit Redacted ersion , September ,

eaknesses are illustrated by EPAs o n records, hich sho several serious computer security incidents since early that have resulted in damage and disruption to agency operations

As a result of these eaknesses, EPAs computer systems and the operations that rely on these systems ere highly vulnerable to tampering, disruption, and misuse from both internal and e ternal sources Moreover, EPA could not ensure the protection of sensitive business and financial data maintained on its larger computer systems or supported by its agency ide net ork

EPA has acted to reduce the e posure of its systems and data and to correct the access control eaknesses e identified E ually important are EPAs efforts to improve its security program planning and management changes that are essential to sustaining the effectiveness of its access controls Our uly report stated that EPAs e isting security program planning and management practices ere largely a paper e ercise that had done little to substantively identify, evaluate, and mitigate risks to the agency s data and systems Accordingly, EPAs planned improvements ill re uire a ma or ad ustment in the ay agency program and technical staff manage the agency s information security risks

epartment of Transportation

The epartment of Transportation OT consists of operating administrations, including the U S Coast Guard, the Federal High ay Administration, the Federal Rail ay Administration, and the Federal Aviation Administration FAA To perform their diverse missions, the OT operating administrations rely on comple infrastructures of computer hard are, soft are, and communications systems At last count, OT had over mission critical systems, including FAA air traffic control systems, Coast Guard search and rescue systems, and financial systems that track billions of federal dollars

In uly , OT s IG reported that revie s of a financial system and net ork systems identified a general lack of background checks on contractor personnel and a lack of appropriate background checks on employees throughout OT The IG also found that the department s systems ere vulnerable to unauthori ed access by Internet users

Interim Report on Computer Security FI , uly ,

In addition, in ecember , e reported that the FAA as not follo ing sound personnel security practices and, as such, had increased the risk that inappropriate individuals may have gained access to its facilities, information, or resources FAAs personnel security policy re uires system o ners and users to prepare risk assessments for all contractor tasks and to conduct background investigations for all contractor employees in high risk positions The policy re uires more limited background checks for moderate and lo risk positions Ho ever, e found that FAA did not perform all the necessary risk assessments and as una are of hether anyone had performed background searches on all of the contractor employees Further, e found instances here background searches ere not performed For e ample, no background searches ere performed on mainland Chinese nationals ho revie ed the source code of eight mission critical systems

In May , e reported that FAA as making progress in implementing its personnel security policy but still needed to complete the re uired background searches for a substantial number of contractor employees We are continuing to evaluate these areas and FAAs overall computer security program

epartment of eterans Affairs

The epartment of eterans Affairs A relies on a vast array of computer systems and telecommunications systems to support its operations and store sensitive information the department collects in carrying out its mission Such operations include financial management, health care delivery, and benefit payments

In September , e reported eaknesses that placed the systems that support these operations at risk of misuse and disruption In October , e reported that A systems continued to be vulnerable to

---

Computer Security FAA Needs to Improve Controls Over Use of Foreign Nationals to Remediate and Revie Soft are GAO AIM , ecember ,

Computer Security FAA Is Addressing Personnel Weaknesses, ut Further Action Is Re uired GAO AIM , May ,

Information Systems A Computer Control Weaknesses Increase Risk of Fraud, Misuse, and Improper isclosure GAO AIM , September

unauthori ed access Specifically, according to our and A IG reports, A had not ade uately limited access of authori ed users or effectively managed user identifications and pass ords and had not properly segregated computer duties As access control eaknesses ere further compounded by ineffective procedures for overseeing and monitoring systems for unusual or suspicious access activities These eaknesses placed sensitive information, including financial data and sensitive veteran medical data and benefit information at increased risk of inadvertent or deliberate misuse, fraudulent use, improper disclosure, or destruction, possibly occurring ithout detection Accordingly, e provided the A ith over recommendations aimed at correcting these problems A has recogni ed the significance of these problems, reporting information security as a material eakness in its Federal Managers Financial Integrity Act FMFIA report for and

One reason for As continuing information system control problems is that the department had not implemented a comprehensive, integrated security management program While A officials had established a central security group and developed and partially implemented an information security program plan, they had not yet developed detailed guidance to ensure that key information security areas highlighted in our October report assessing risk, monitoring system and user access activity, and evaluating the effectiveness of information system controls ere fully addressed and consistently implemented throughout the department The department plans to implement additional security initiatives by May and establish a fully operational security program by anuary

epartment of Agriculture

In uly , e reported that the epartment of Agriculture s National Finance Center NFC had serious access control eaknesses that affected its ability to prevent or detect unauthori ed changes to payroll and other payment data or computer soft are NFC is responsible for processing billions of dollars in payroll payments for hundreds of thousands of federal employees and maintaining records for the orld s largest k type program Specifically, NFC had not sufficiently restricted access authority for legitimate users In one instance, users identifications had an access

Information Systems The Status of Computer Security at the epartment of eterans Affairs GAO AIM , October

US A Information Security Weaknesses at National Finance Center Increase Risk of Fraud, Misuse, and Improper isclosure GAO AIM , uly , privilege that allo s users to read and alter any data tape, including payroll files, regardless of other security soft are controls In addition, mainframe computer users had been granted privileges that allo ed them to access sensitive operating system files, including audit trail information Further, NFC had not ade uately established security policies and procedures that addressed all aspects of NFC s interconnected environment or implemented a process to measure, test, and report on the effectiveness of computer controls

In August , the epartment of Agriculture IG reported that, hile the NFC had completed corrective actions on of technical eaknesses e had identified, eaknesses, pertaining to logical access controls, had not been corrected In addition, the IG found that NFC had not implemented an entity ide security program as e had recommended

Other Federal Operations

In une , e testified that the epartment of State, hile taking several positive steps, had not ade uately addressed previously reported access control and security program management eaknesses Our revie found that State still needed to take steps to ensure that all audit recommendations and identified security vulnerabilities are addressed, e pand its automated intrusion detection program, and further clarify agency ide security management responsibilities
In May , based on a survey of federal agencies, e reported that controls over changes to soft are for federal information systems as described in agency policies and procedures ere inade uate Specifically, e found that in many cases formally documented policies and procedures did not e ist or did not meet the re uirements of federal criteria, oversight of contractors as inade uate, especially hen soft are change functions ere completely contracted out, and background screenings of personnel involved in the soft are change process ere not a routine security control Such

Revie of Corrective Actions Taken by the National Finance Center on General Accounting Office Recommendations in Report GAO AIM , dated uly , , Memorandum from US A IG to US A Chief Financial Officer, August ,

Foreign Affairs Effort to Upgrade Information Technology Overseas Faces Formidable Challenges GAO T AIM NSIA , une ,

Information Security Controls Over Soft are Changes at Federal Agencies GAO AIM R, May ,

eaknesses increase the risks that untrust orthy and untrained individuals could have unrestricted access to soft are code, security features could be inadvertently or deliberately omitted or rendered inoperable, processing irregularities could occur, or malicious code could be introduced We suggested many remedies for the eaknesses e identified, and officials at many of the agencies told us that they had begun to implement them

Although Nature of Risks aries, Control Weaknesses Across Agencies Are Similar

The nature of agency operations and the related risks vary Ho ever, as e reported in September , there are striking similarities in the specific types of general control eaknesses reported and in their serious negative impact on an agency s ability to ensure the integrity, availability, and appropriate confidentiality of its computeri ed operations The follo ing sections describe each of the si areas of general controls and the specific eaknesses that ere most idespread at the agencies covered by our analysis

Entity ide Security Program Planning and Management

Each organi ation needs a set of management procedures and an organi ational frame ork for identifying and assessing risks, deciding hat policies and controls are needed, periodically evaluating the effectiveness of these policies and controls, and acting to address any identified eaknesses These are the fundamental activities that allo an organi ation to manage its information security risks cost effectively, rather than react to individual problems in an ad hoc manner only after a violation has been detected or an audit finding has been reported

espite the importance of this aspect of an information security program, poor security planning and management continues to be a idespread problem As noted earlier, of the agencies for hich this aspect of security as revie ed, all had deficiencies Many of these agencies had not developed security plans for ma or systems based on risk, had not documented security policies, and had not implemented a program for testing and evaluating the effectiveness of the controls they relied on As a result, agencies ere not fully a are of the information security risks to their operations, had accepted an unkno n level of risk by default rather than consciously deciding hat level of risk as tolerable, had a false sense of security because they ere relying on controls that ere not effective, and could not make informed udgments as to hether they ere spending too little or too much of their resources on security

Access Controls

Access controls limit or detect inappropriate access to computer resources data, e uipment, and facilities thereby protecting these resources against unauthori ed modification, loss, and disclosure Access controls include physical protections, such as gates and guards, as ell as logical controls, hich are controls built into soft are that re uire users to authenticate themselves through the use of secret pass ords or other identifiers and limit the files and other resources that an authenticated user can access and the actions that he or she can e ecute Without ade uate access controls, unauthori ed individuals, including outside intruders and terminated employees, can surreptitiously read and copy sensitive data and make undetected changes or deletions for malicious purposes or personal gain In addition, authori ed users could unintentionally modify or delete data or e ecute changes that are outside of their span of authority

For access controls to be effective, they must be properly implemented and maintained First, an organi ation must analy e the responsibilities of individual computer users to determine hat type of access e g , read, modify, delete they need to fulfill their responsibilities Then, specific control techni ues, such as speciali ed access control soft are, must be implemented to restrict access to these authori ed functions Such soft are can be used to limit a user s activities associated ith specific systems or files and to keep records of individual user s actions on the computer Finally, access authori ations and related controls must be maintained and ad usted on an ongoing basis to accommodate ne and terminated employees and changes in users responsibilities and related access needs

Access controls ere evaluated at all of the agencies covered by our revie , and significant eaknesses ere reported for each of these , as evidenced by the follo ing e amples

Agencies had not implemented effective user account and pass ord management practices to reduce the risk that accounts could be used to gain unauthori ed system access E amples include the follo ing
Accounts and pass ords for individuals no longer associated ith the agency ere not deleted or disabled
Users did not periodically change their pass ords
Access as not promptly terminated hen users either left the agency or ad usted hen their responsibilities no longer re uired them to have access to certain files
Inactive user identifications ere not routinely identified and deleted As a result, contractors and former employees ho ere no

longer associated ith the agency could still read, modify, copy, or delete data, and employees ho changed positions ithin an agency had access to files that ere not needed in their ne positions At one agency, an individual no longer officially affiliated ith the agency gained access to an agency computer and altered the access privileges, indicating a serious eakness in the agency s process for applying changes in personnel status to computer accounts At another agency, individuals, mostly contractor employees, ho ere no longer orking for the agency still retained access to agency systems, and some accounts ere used after the individuals left agency employment Also at this agency, , of , users ere not deleted after days of inactivity

Managers had not precisely identified access needs for individual users or groups of users Instead, they had provided overly broad access privileges to very large groups of users As a result, far more individuals than necessary had the ability to bro se and, sometimes, modify or delete sensitive or critical information At one agency, all , users ere granted access to sensitive system directories and settings

Access as not appropriately authori ed and documented For e ample, at one agency, , users had been provided access to one system ithout ritten authori ation

Use of default, easily guessed, and unencrypted pass ords significantly increased the risk of unauthori ed access uring testing at one agency, e ere able to guess many pass ords based on our kno ledge of commonly used pass ords and ere able to observe computer users keying in pass ords and then use those pass ords to obtain high level system administration privileges

Soft are access controls ere improperly implemented, resulting in unintended access or gaps in access control coverage At one agency data center, all users, including programmers and computer operators, had the capability to read sensitive production data, increasing the risk that sensitive information could be disclosed to unauthori ed individuals Also, at this agency, certain users had the unrestricted ability to transfer system files across the net ork, increasing the risk that unauthori ed individuals could gain access to the sensitive data or programs At another agency, user accounts had been granted privileges enabling them to change program code ithout supervisory revie or approval

User activity as not ade uately monitored to deter and identify inappropriate actions At one agency, much of the activity associated ith our intrusion testing as not recogni ed and recorded, and the problem reports that ere recorded did not recogni e the magnitude of our activity or the severity of the security breaches e initiated

To illustrate the risks associated ith poor authentication and access controls, in recent years e have begun to incorporate penetration testing into our audits of information security Such tests involve attempting, ith agency cooperation, to gain unauthori ed access to sensitive files and data by searching for ays to circumvent e isting controls, often from remote locations As e reported in   , our auditors have been successful, in almost every test, in readily gaining unauthori ed access that ould allo intruders to read, modify, or delete data for hatever purpose they had in mind

Application Soft are evelopment and Change Controls

Application soft are development and change controls prevent unauthori ed soft are programs or modifications to programs from being implemented ey aspects of such controls are ensuring that soft are changes are properly authori ed by the managers responsible for the agency program or operations that the application supports, ne and modified soft are programs are tested and approved prior to their implementation, and approved soft are programs are maintained in carefully controlled libraries to protect them from unauthori ed changes and to ensure that different versions are not misidentified

Such controls can prevent both errors in soft are programming as ell as malicious efforts to insert unauthori ed computer program code Without ade uate controls, incompletely tested or unapproved soft are can result in erroneous data processing that, depending on the application, could lead to losses or faulty outcomes In addition, individuals could surreptitiously modify soft are programs to include processing steps or features that could later be e ploited for personal gain or sabotage

Weaknesses in soft are program change controls ere identified for of the agencies here such controls ere evaluated E amples of eaknesses in this area included the follo ing

Testing procedures ere undisciplined and did not ensure that implemented soft are operated as intended For e ample, at one agency, senior officials authori ed some systems for processing ithout testing access controls to ensure that they had been implemented and ere operating effectively At another, documentation as not retained to demonstrate user testing and acceptance

Implementation procedures did not ensure that only authori ed soft are as used In particular, procedures did not ensure that emergency changes ere subse uently tested and formally approved for continued use and that implementation of locally developed unauthori ed soft are programs as prevented or detected Agencies policies and procedures fre uently did not address the maintenance and protection of program libraries

Segregation of uties

Segregation of duties refers to the policies, procedures, and organi ational structure that help ensure that one individual cannot independently control all key aspects of a process or computer related operation and thereby conduct unauthori ed actions or gain unauthori ed access to assets or records ithout detection For e ample, one computer programmer should not be allo ed to independently rite, test, and approve program changes

Although segregation of duties, alone, ill not ensure that only authori ed activities occur, inade uate segregation of duties increases the risk that erroneous or fraudulent transactions could be processed, that improper program changes could be implemented, and that computer resources could be damaged or destroyed For e ample,

an individual ho as independently responsible for authori ing, processing, and revie ing payroll transactions could inappropriately increase payments to selected individuals ithout detection or

a computer programmer responsible for authori ing, riting, testing, and distributing program modifications could either inadvertently or deliberately implement computer programs that did not process transactions in accordance ith management s policies or that included malicious code

Controls to ensure appropriate segregation of duties consist mainly of documenting, communicating, and enforcing policies on group and individual responsibilities Enforcement can be accomplished by a combination of physical and logical access controls and by effective supervisory revie

Segregation of duties as evaluated at of the agencies covered by our analysis, and eaknesses ere identified at of these agencies Common problems involved computer programmers and operators ho ere authori ed to perform a ide variety of duties, thus providing them the ability to independently modify, circumvent, and disable system security features For e ample, at one data center, a single individual could independently develop, test, revie , and approve soft are changes for implementation

Segregation of duty problems also ere identified related to transaction processing For e ample, at one agency, staff involved ith procurement had system access privileges that allo ed them to individually re uest, approve, and record the receipt of purchased items In addition, of the staff had system access privileges that allo ed them to edit the vendor file, hich could result in fictitious vendors being added to the file for fraudulent purposes For fiscal year , e identified purchases, totaling about , , that ere re uested, approved, and receipt recorded by the same individual

System Soft are Controls

System soft are controls limit and monitor access to the po erful programs and sensitive files associated ith the computer systems operation Generally, one set of system soft are is used to support and control a variety of applications that may run on the same computer hard are System soft are helps control and coordinate the input, processing, output, and data storage associated ith all of the applications that run on the system Some system soft are can change data and program code on files ithout leaving an audit trail or can be used to modify or delete audit trails E amples of system soft are include the operating system, system utilities, program library systems, file maintenance soft are, security soft are, data communications systems, and database management systems

Controls over access to and modification of system soft are are essential in providing reasonable assurance that operating system based security controls are not compromised and that the system ill not be impaired If controls in this area are inade uate, unauthori ed individuals might use system soft are to circumvent security controls to read, modify, or delete critical or sensitive information and programs Also, authori ed users of the system may gain unauthori ed privileges to conduct unauthori ed actions or to circumvent edits and other controls built into application programs Such eaknesses seriously diminish the reliability of information produced by all of the applications supported by the computer system and increase the risk of fraud, sabotage, and inappropriate disclosures Further, system soft are programmers are often more technically proficient than other data processing personnel and, thus, have a greater ability to perform unauthori ed actions if controls in this area are eak

The control concerns for system soft are are similar to the access control issues and soft are program change control issues discussed earlier in this section Ho ever, because of the high level of risk associated ith system soft are activities, most entities have a separate set of control procedures that apply to them

Operating system soft are controls ere covered in audits for of the agencies included in our revie This as a significant increase over , hen e reported that this important control area had been revie ed for only agencies

Weaknesses ere identified at each of the agencies for hich operating system controls ere revie ed A common type of problem reported as insufficiently restricted access that made it possible for kno ledgeable individuals to disable or circumvent controls in a ide variety of ays For e ample, at one agency, system support personnel had the ability to change data in the system audit log As a result, they could have engaged in a ide array of inappropriate and unauthori ed activity and could have subse uently deleted related segments of the audit log, thus diminishing the likelihood that their actions ould be detected

Service Continuity Controls

Service continuity controls ensure that, hen une pected events occur, critical operations continue ithout undue interruption and that critical and sensitive data are protected For this reason, an agency should have procedures in place to protect information resources and minimi e the risk of unplanned interruptions and a plan to recover critical operations should interruptions occur These plans should consider the activities performed at general support facilities, such as data processing centers, as ell as the activities performed by users of specific applications To determine hether recovery plans ill ork as intended, they should be tested periodically in disaster simulation e ercises

Controls to ensure service continuity should address the entire range of potential disruptions These may include relatively minor interruptions, such as temporary po er failures or accidental loss or erasure of files, as ell as ma or disasters, such as fires or natural disasters that ould re uire reestablishing operations at a remote location

osing the capability to process, retrieve, and protect information maintained electronically can significantly affect an agency s ability to accomplish its mission If controls are inade uate, even relatively minor interruptions can result in lost or incorrectly processed data, hich can cause financial losses, e pensive recovery efforts, and inaccurate or incomplete financial or management information Service continuity controls include   taking steps, such as routinely making backup copies of files, to prevent and minimi e potential damage and interruption,   developing and documenting a comprehensive contingency plan, and   periodically testing the contingency plan and ad usting it as appropriate

Service continuity controls ere evaluated for   of the   of the agencies included in our analysis Of these   , eaknesses ere reported for   agencies E amples of eaknesses included the follo ing

   Plans ere incomplete because operations and supporting resources had not been fully analy ed to determine hich ere the most critical and ould need to be resumed as soon as possible should a disruption occur
   isaster recovery plans ere not fully tested to identify their eaknesses At one agency, periodic alkthroughs or unannounced tests of the disaster recovery plan had not been performed Conducting these types of test provides a scenario more likely to be encountered in the event of an actual disaster

Conclusions

The e panded body of audit evidence that has become available since   e reported on the status of federal information security in September   sho s that important operations at every ma or federal agency continue to be at risk as a result of eak information security controls There are many specific causes of these eaknesses, but an underlying problem is poor security program management and poor administration of available control techni ues While agencies have taken steps to address problems and many have remedial efforts under ay, audits completed over the past year sho   that agencies have not implemented fundamental management practices needed to ensure that their computer based controls remain effective on an ongoing basis

The audit reports cited in this report include many recommendations to individual agencies that address the specific eaknesses reported For this reason, e are making no additional recommendations to these agencies in this report Ho ever, e have issued t o e ecutive guides that discuss practices that leading organi ations have employed to strengthen the effectiveness of their security programs These e ecutive guides are

Information Security Management   earning From eading Organi ations   GAO AIM   , May   and Information Security Risk Assessment Practices of eading Organi ations GAO AIM   , November

As agreed ith your office, unless you publicly announce the contents of this report earlier, e plan no further distribution until   days from the date of this letter At that time, e ill send copies to The Honorable acob   e , irector of the Office of Management and udget, and the Heads, Chief Information Officers, and Inspectors General of the   federal departments and agencies covered by our revie   We are also sending copies to the Chairs and Ranking Minority Members of the Senate Governmental Affairs Committee and the House Committee on Government Reform, as ell as to other interested members of the Congress Copies ill be made available to others upon re uest

If you have any uestions regarding this report, please contact me at   or by e mail at *daceyr aimd gao gov*

Sincerely yours,

Robert F acey
 irector
Information Security Issues

Ob ectives, Scope, and Methodology

Our ob ectives ere to   analy e and summari e information security
 eaknesses identified in audit reports issued from uly   through
August   and compare these findings ith similar information that e
reported in September   ,   identify e amples of eaknesses and the
related risks at selected individual agencies, and   identify the most
significant types of eaknesses in each of si categories of general controls
that e used in our analysis

We analy ed findings from over   GAO and agency reports, including
inspector general reports, issued from uly   through August   The
reports e considered pertained to the   federal departments and
agencies covered by the Chief Financial Officers Act Together these
departments and agencies accounted for about   percent of the total
reported federal net outlays in fiscal year

In analy ing reported findings, e categori ed them into si basic areas of
general control security program planning and management, access
control, application program change control, segregation of duties,
operating systems security, and service continuity These si areas of
general controls provide a frame ork for comprehensively evaluating
information security that is described in GAO s *Federal Information
Systems Controls Audit Manual*

Our analysis as performed during August   in accordance ith
generally accepted government auditing standards

GAO Contacts and Staff Ackno ledgments

GAO Contact

ean olt , , bolt aimd gao gov

Ackno ledgments

Other ma or contributors to this ork ere ebra Conner, ohn de Ferrari, avid Irvin, Eli abeth ohnston, Sharon ittrell, effrey nott, Carol angelier, Colleen Phillips, Alicia Sommers, Cra ford Thompson, William Thompson, and Gregory Wilshusen